SUSTAINABLE YOU

8 First Steps To Lasting Change In Business And In Life

MICHAEL PRAGER

FISHERBLUE PRESS • ARLINGTON

Sustainable YOU

8 First Steps to Lasting Change in
Business and in Life

© 2016 Michael Prager
Fisherblue Press
ISBN 978-0-9826720-2-0

Contact:
Michael Prager
781-951-2411
30 Fisher Road, Arlington, MA 02476 USA

Michael@MichaelPrager.com
MichaelPrager.com

Printed in the United States of America

This book is for all the people, peers and professionals, who shared their experiences and knowledge with me, including Bob Deutsch, Linda Boynton, Phil Werdell and Mary Foushi, Vivian and Flo who went by first names only at the rehab hospital. They set me on a path to better places, most of them wholly unexpected, one of which was this book. Thank you, thank you, thank you.

Contents

Foreword

We've all done it, I'm sure. Whether it is for the annual New Year's resolution ritual, the spring rush to fit into that swimsuit, or the fifth time trying to quit tobacco, we all have tried to change a behavior and then felt the guilt when it didn't work. It's a never-ending cycle of try, try again.

When Michael asked me to write the foreword for *Sustainable You,* I found myself recalling all my own failed attempts to shake off some bad habit or extra pounds. It struck me that my biggest problem comes from not being able to sustain the new behaviors, while falling back into those I am most comfortable with. *Sustainable YOU* guides us in taking steps to analyze our behaviors, challenge the processes we have set up to run amok, and seek out a more sustainable set of practices that get us to a better place.

I have been fortunate to learn from someone who fished (legally) with a net, which is a surprisingly intricate process. It is a carefully choreographed maneuver accounting for wind direction and speed, water movement, and the position of the school of fish. Once the net is lofted into the air, allowing the wind to open it to its fullest volume, the net collapses into the water, and over the school. With yet another move of agility and planning, the fisher not only draws the net back to the boat with some fish, but does so such that the net folds under itself setting a sort of cup-like trap for fish. This process is repeated on each side of the boat, moving the boat around the area as the school moves, until the fisher reaches the catch limit or is called home.

We, who deliver wellness programming to our employees/colleagues, can take a lesson from the net fisher. Wellness, like the net, needs to be a carefully choreographed set of programs that are "thrown" or "tossed" out to the employee population with consistency and repetition despite the number of employees that may latch on.

Herein lies the first challenge with wellness programming to date: We give up the moment engagement drops. I would submit that we need to do the opposite and keep providing, a la "casting the net." Under some models, behavior change is a combination of the desire to change, as in on the part of the employee here, and the need to maintain the alternative behaviors to sustain the change. So, not unlike the fisher and the net, wellness programs cannot simply stop out of frustration or lack of participation. Instead, they must sustain their presence and provide the net for employees when they are at their behavior-change moment.

We need to prepare the programs thoughtfully. A hasty or overly complicated program roll-out can destroy both that program and the integrity of the entire wellness initiative. Complex and difficult-to-access programs turn off users.

If you run, or are part of, an employer offering of wellness programs, remember: 1) Prepare your net with care; 2) Cast your net wide, often, and consistently; 3) Don't stop casting; 4) Repeat steps 1-3. As Michael shows us in *Sustainable YOU*, small steps — when thought about, digested, and implemented — can lead to lasting change. So read this book and do the activities after each section. In the end you will be better off and think a bit more before you fall back into that bad behavior.

Thomas A. Sondergeld
Vice President Global Benefits & Mobility
Walgreens Boots Alliance

Acknowledgments

My foremost supporter on the planet is my spouse and closest friend, Georgina Fulton Prager, and like so many of the best things in my life, this book would not exist without her.

I have also been helped by a series of professionals whose services I am grateful for:

- Editor and, well, book-runner Claudia Gere. I was telling audiences at the beginning of 2014 that this book would be out by midyear. I missed that expectation by more than a year, but I don't think it would be complete even now (whenever you're reading this) without Claudia's help. Good ideas, good vibes, and well suited to share them.

- Damaris Curran Herlihy, owner of Curran Press and Editorial Consulting, LLC. Damaris provided key guidance, editing prowess, and encouragement.

- David Richwine, the first copy editor I seek out for any job.

- Pete Weissman. A fellow member of the National Speakers Association, Pete has been both exceedingly sharp and generous with his time and expertise. Joe Veneto, too, has been extraordinary among many NSA-ers who've helped me.

- Michael Rothenberg, owner of Peak Productions. Michael is very skilled, very supportive, and very generous. He has produced videos for me.

- Photographer Bethany Versoy. Her work appears on the back cover. If you know me, you know she makes me look better than I do look.

Change the World or Change Yourself?

If you had to, which would you choose? One could argue for either, but the best answer is: "You don't have to choose." They're two sides of one idea.

I'm so passionate about this intimate connection that I proclaim it all the time — in speaking engagements, on my blog, and on these pages. In the chapters that follow, I'll detail eight concepts that define this route, which I've coined "sustainable personal change." But first, I want to share the two threads of my experience that led to my identifying these concepts.

Path to Weight Loss

The longer of the two tales has been developing for most of my years — 57 as of this writing. For about 30 years, I was so overweight that at one point I signed myself into the eating disorders unit of a psychiatric hospital. One of the first facts I learned is that I didn't really understand my problem!

I thought my problem was weight gain, and of course that was part of it. But my excess weight was evidence of a problem, not the problem itself. Up to that point, I'd lost more than 300 pounds, proof that I was a champion dieter. But I was exactly like the smoker who said, "Quit? Sure! Done it plenty of times."

Somewhere in the mid-1980s, I stumbled onto a path that has now afforded me a normal-sized body for almost a quarter-century — although even to say "stumbled" gives me too much credit. The best I can claim is that I wanted to escape the results of my choices. In addition to rehab, this path has included individual and group therapy, as well as substantial time in support groups. The journey hasn't been effortless, but escape rarely is.

My first shove toward this new direction came from a supervisor who suggested that I undergo therapy, and — haltingly, via the company's employee assistance program — I did. Things didn't click with the first two therapists they sent me to, but then I was referred to Dr. Bob Deutsch of West Hartford, Connecticut. I didn't give him an easy time, but he broke through my defenses, and I've been living on the spoils of his victory ever since.

Interpersonally, I've gone from almost undatable to the married father of a 5-year-old. What makes the transition remarkable is that I didn't have my first girlfriend until age 36 — as good a measure as any of my disaffection from general society.

Professionally, I went from erratic to dependable. In my 20s, I held a high rank at the Hartford newspaper where I worked, but was soon demoted because I couldn't get along with others. If I had departed the paper in that timeframe, the only celebration by my colleagues would have come after I'd gone. But when I did leave a couple years later to help edit The Boston Globe, friends held two going-away parties — and I was invited to both.

During my 14 years at the Globe, I held several nice positions, including chief of a section. I also returned to writing in earnest, on the side. When I left, it was to be a stay-at-home dad, a prospect that materialized far later than my wife and I expected.

Path to Community

While we were waiting to start a family, I was drawn, quite organically, to cover the sustainability movement. I began going to "green" trade shows and writing for magazines such as GreenSource and E — The Environmental Magazine.

But just like with the weight, I spent considerable time working to fix the sustainability problem before I came to realize that I didn't really understand what it was.

I thought the problem was that nature simply wasn't cooperating with human plans, and that the solution was to use new materials to rebuild all the stuff we'd built wrong. I've now concluded I erred on both counts.

Today, I'd say that sustainability — quite literally, the ability to sustain — is the primary challenge of every life on the planet. To evaluate that statement, I suggest we make a list of all the people, groups, and species that didn't have the ability to sustain, and what we'll have is the list of those that failed the sustainability challenge.

Meanwhile, it's laughable to think that it's nature's job to cooperate with our intentions. If you think of Earth's existence as one 24-hour period, nature arrived before dawn, and we appeared about a minute before midnight. Is nature a part of humankind, or is humankind a part of nature?

Ask Nature

I would soon see the same disconnect in a different context. But first, I needed to learn about biomimicry, an approach born with the hunter-gatherers but whose modern roots grew from the 1997 publication of Janine Benyus's book Biomimicry: Innovation Inspired by Nature. Its guiding idea is that nature has solved most of the design and building problems that humans encounter. Instead of trying to defeat the natural processes that annoy us, we should look to nature for solutions we can mimic.

For example, humans want to live in many climatic and geographical environments such as deserts, flood plains, and mountaintops, so we've devised resource-hungry systems to make it possible. They work, but at significant cost. For example, utilities need fuel to provide us with electricity, but unearthing coal disfigures the land, blackens the water, and soils the air.

In contrast, for the Eastgate Centre development in Harare, Zimbabwe, Australian architect Mick Pearce adapted the natural ventilation properties of termite mounds to vastly reduce mechanical heating and cooling, despite the city's subtropical highlands climate. (The website asknature.org offers countless other biomimicry examples.)

I am drawn to these ideas by their elegance, as I think most people would be. Even though I didn't begin to consider the idea until I had turned 50, the notion of looking to nature for solutions seems obvious.

In fact, I soon began wondering: Should we apply principles of nature to the architecture of our lives, as well as the architecture of our structures? Turns out following nature will help our lives, too.

For example, when I was unhealthy and overweight, I was lonely, but still practiced isolation — in conflict with the universal urge to be among others. I was an outsized case, both physically and otherwise. But to some degree, I was just being American. As a nation, we venerate the rugged individualist, we seek our own chunk of land, we'd rather drive ourselves to work than commute with others.

Nature, meanwhile, models community in several ways. The herd instinct, for example, is one in which the safest place is in the middle, surrounded by one's peers. Ecosystem is another word for communities in which each part does better when all parts are healthy. Symbiosis describes communities of two: Both members thrive by making the other's life possible.

Looking back, I can see now that my path out of trouble used several forms of community. Two were the therapy and support groups. Another important example was my surrendering my conviction that I needed nobody else's help to get better. The laughable part of that contention is that I claimed my opinions arose from my powers of intellect, logic, and observation. But if those powers had been reliable, I would easily have seen that evidence did not support my conclusions!

I started to see what I wasn't seeing by hanging out in support groups. I also got to observe how others dealt with similar deficits, and grudgingly consented to allow some whom I considered worthy to guide me. Just conceding that "if I'm so smart, how did I end up in rehab?" was enough to nudge me forward.

Coming from imperiousness and isolation to engaging in community was life-changing. But eventually, I ran up against its limits. Other people, especially those to whom I could specifically relate, definitely had information for me. But they could not solve my every dilemma, choose for me at every crossroads, make bearable every hurt. Not only were they humans, like me, prone to error and a bad day, but I had met my peer advisers in institutions, and they, too, were seeking help with their deficits and dysfunctions.

In some ways, I relied on consensus from the group as I could perceive it over time, on the belief that if I couldn't or shouldn't rely on any one person, I could benefit from its accumulated wisdom. I was particularly unhappy with a recurring theme not only endorsed, but strongly suggested — that I develop a spiritual life.

Before I could even explore such a thing, I'd have to overcome prejudices calcified in childhood — not only my aforementioned reliance on logic, but also my certainty that spirituality and religion were different names for one entity.

I could not understand why, for example, innocent children could be run over by their parents' cars in a world guided by some benevolent superpower. My error there, I believe now, was to expect that I should be able to understand everything in a very complex system where quite a lot is not understandable.

Why does electricity work? Why doesn't the atmosphere blow away? Why is there no Channel 1? I couldn't explain any of them. But on the existence of a deeper power, I required an answer — or God was just an asshole.

Of course, I also maintained that God didn't exist, and how could that be? Only a God-like power could be anything and nothing, all at once.

In the pages that follow, we'll explore these and other questions by examining eight concepts I've culled from my experiences for sustaining personal change. I don't claim that these are the only principles of personal sustainability, nor do I present them as a package deal. Apply what seems reasonable to you, in any combination or order. Here's an introduction:

   ☐ It's All One Thing: The interconnectedness of all life is both undeniable and valuable as a guide to individual conduct.

   ☐ It's Never Just One Thing: Egged on by advertisers, many of us think we can solve everything with that one "right" change, but it's never that simple.

   ☐ It Matters: What you and I do, individually, on a daily basis, has a strong effect on both ourselves and on the world. A look at why so many act otherwise.

☐ Working Together Is a Selfish Act: Of course it's true that engaging effectively in community benefits the community, but the individuals who engage benefit greatly, too.

☐ Working Together Isn't Enough: Combining with others is necessary, but not sufficient, because as rewarding as that is, it relies on human power alone, and at least some of the time, something deeper is required.

☐ Not Everything Has to Make Sense: Logic is useful and powerful, but try explaining a paradox. That only begins the case for going beyond logic to decide how to conduct ourselves.

☐ If You've Had Enough, Have You Done Enough? The attitude that "[X] ought to be enough" is overvalued. The only value "ought" has in the process of change is a negative one. The only credible standard for "enough" is when your goal begins to materialize.

☐ Change Is a Choice: Others' desires for you to change are meaningless annoyances until you decide you want to change. Once you commit, it's a simple matter of follow-through.

Finally, an aside for those who might wonder why I often write in the first person. Contrary to how it may appear, I do not think this is all about me-me-me. I use the first person because while I believe my experiences can entertain, inform, and inspire others, I am talking strictly about my experiences, rather than claiming that I know yours. It is your call to determine what, if any of it, is applicable to you. I can't depend on always knowing what's best for me, but I can depend on rarely knowing what's best for you.

CONCEPT 1

It's All One Thing

The point of this chapter is wholism, nothing less. But before getting to it, let's start with ... the spelling?

The dictionaries prefer "holism," but to me, that spelling connotes alternative (as in "not really") medicine, perhaps favored by remainders of the '60s counterculture and others but discounted by most. Spelled "wholism," the concept is not only freed of that freight, but it readily suggests "whole," which is better. "Wholism" also avoids any hint of "holy," which stems from a different root than "holism" but still evokes it.

No matter the spelling, Merriam-Webster defines the term as "a theory that the universe and especially living nature is correctly seen in terms of interacting wholes (as of living organisms) that are more than the mere sum of elementary particles."

This is one of the foundational facts of life, and yet, for my first few decades, I didn't so much deny it as live in ignorance of it. My overweight condition was only the most obvious example.

Like most people unhappy with being overweight, I thought the solution was a diet. That was wrong from several perspectives, but the germane portion here is that I was looking at a symptom of a systemic problem, but thought it was the problem.

Being overweight was a problem, unquestionably, and yes, I needed to change how I ate. But attacking a systemic problem with a short-term solution — as dieting is universally regarded — can only fail. And yet, hundreds of millions of people worldwide turn first, and usually only, to dieting. Clearly I hadn't been the only one making this mistake.

Connected to the World "Out There"

Perhaps it stretches the concept of connectedness, but it's fair to say that we, the mistaken, were connected by our common misapprehension. I'm willing to stretch it in this case because, of the two extremes, we far more undervalue the undeniable connections — to ourselves, to everyone, to all life — than we overstate it.

And how? How can that be, when our interconnection is not only broad, but deep. Here are a few examples.

Our bodies are made up principally of six elements — oxygen, carbon, hydrogen, nitrogen, calcium, and phosphorus — with traces of five others. All of it comes from space, going back to the beginning of time. We are, not just prosaically but literally, created from stardust. Every person on earth, on average, is 99.5 percent similar chemically to every other person. No two are identical, not even identical twins, but we could hardly be more alike.

Earth is essentially a closed system, so anything we consume came from something someone else consumed before. As a colorful hydrologist friend told me, "we're all drinking dinosaur piss."

Likewise, the decisions we make have intense effects on the planet and on one another. The burning of fossil fuels is raising sea levels, imperiling lowlands everywhere — including the Maldives Islands nation, whose highest point is only about 8 feet above sea level. It's correct that the car you drove to work this morning is not, individually, going to cause this Indian Ocean nation to disappear. But if we weren't burning fossil fuels, the Maldives wouldn't be threatened. We each have a share in that reality, even if the shares are very small.

Our effect spreads further than just to other humans, of course. Our choices affect other species, sometimes to the point of dooming them or ourselves. Consider the decline of bees, which are deemed essential to our food supply. Although science is still determining the exact cause, many scientists blame the widespread use of pesticides.

Quite literally, quite undeniably, the choices we make have consequences. We can deny this reality. We can explain it away, blaming forces out of our control. But these consequences happen regardless. We are endlessly interconnected, and yet how many of us even nod to this condition?

Connected to Our Immediate World

So far, I've painted the connection picture in strokes of species, planets, and the gene pool, and even where we can see the effects on the world of our individual choices, it's still pretty easy to regard the world as "out there," not having to do with us personally. Perhaps, in a world of 8.7 million species, when just our species has 7.1 billion members, that's understandable.

But what explains its corollary, that many of us don't feel we have much effect on our own lives? The platinum examples are smoking and obesity. The debate over whether smoking will degrade, then shorten, one's life is completely over, and yet 800 million earthlings still choose to inhale — even at a cost, in the United States, of more than $5 a pack. Paying through the nose to ruin one's lungs can only be explained if users don't think they will experience the obvious result of their choices.

I used to be one of those: I smoked cigarettes for 14 years, and have reached dependence on cigars a couple of times since. (The canard that cigars are "OK," because one doesn't inhale, certainly is not true for me.) And of course, I took myself to an extreme of body size, while maintaining that it didn't matter in my life.

And that was true, except that part about how it was the biggest factor in my life! Not only my body size, but my self-image, my fitness, my social life, my ability to function at work, and so on. I recall visiting an Acura dealer while shopping for a car. As I struggled to squeeze into the Integra, I recall telling the salesman: "It looks like a problem, but it really isn't." There was the whole tale, in miniature.

For most of my life, I never even considered whether these topics — planet-level conditions (which, like most people, I held under the heading of sustainability) and personal habits — had any connection. Then came the time when I needed them to have one, after I'd built a blog on sustainability while publishing a book about food addiction.

I'd risen to about 3,000 hits a month before realizing that if "Fat Boy Thin Man" was to survive in the marketplace, I'd have to support it with a blog, among other tools. I knew I couldn't support two blogs, so I was either going to have to abandon my baby or figure out how food addiction made sense under the "SUSTAINABLY" banner.

Here's what I went with initially: Obesity is absolutely a sustainability issue, both for individuals and for the planet. For the former, it is exhausting to expend so much time, energy, money, and focus to maintain what is, almost universally, an unnatural body size. For the latter, regard the resources being spent on the extra food that keeps 2 billion people worldwide either obese or overweight.

Both rationales are true, but at the time, even driven by the selfish push of commercial survival, I had trouble convincing myself.

Slowly, though, I saw the parallels between my misconceptions around weight and around what I perceived to be sustainability — that in the former, the answer was a diet, and in the latter it was green tech. Both had truth in them — I needed to eat very differently, and we needed to build very differently — but both were pointed at what only appeared to be the problem.

In both cases, the all-too-human error was thinking that my choices and those of others would not have the only effects that they had! Yes, I did somehow separate the fact that I was eating to excess, every day, from the fact that I didn't want the effects that overeating had on my body.

And yes, even consumers more enlightened than the AC-while-the-car-windows-are-open crowd might have bought low-consumption (and mercury-containing) lightbulbs, but they'll still fly in an airplane as the need arises and own a crossover or 4-by-4, feeling justified "because my other car's a Prius."

(For this discussion, it's only an aside, but despite having surrendered most processed foods for more than a decade, and driving a Prius past 130,000 miles, I do not feel deprived on either count. I didn't talk myself into either of these, either. Meanwhile, this is a good place to disclose that we also own a station wagon, and we are imperfect in just about every planet-friendly consideration.)

I don't know why we perceive this disconnection from the effects our choices have, either on our own lives or on the world at large. But I offer evidence that it has existed for a very long time, as in, "In the beginning..." In Genesis 1:28, one of the best-known Bible verses, we are told that humans have "dominion over the fish of the sea, and over the fowl of the air, and over every living thing that moveth upon the earth ..."

The passage's standard interpretation is that we have a responsibility for Earth's inhabitants, and I don't disagree. But does it not draw a line between us and all other life on the planet? As if it's them versus us? As if the physical laws don't apply to us, too?

Why Does It Matter?

Even those who would concede the truth behind these points may still react, "So what? Why should I bother even to change my local impact, never mind all that world-level crap? It's hard, and I've got a job, a family, and plans this weekend."

Indeed, that is the question. Few people change without good reason — I didn't — and to paraphrase an observation most sparkling, most people are willing to surrender what they want for what they want now. (I'd love to attribute the notion, but haven't been able to find who said it.)

Here's my answer: By reconsidering what was worth my attention and what wasn't, my life has become substantially better. And since I'm sure I'm just another Joe on the bus, I'm convinced that shifting one's actions according to his or her own self-interest, redefined in this way, can bring the same result.

Please note that I'm not saying, "You will lose weight too." How would I even know if you need that? The primary example from my experience is weight loss, but these ideas are about change, not weight loss. To emphasize the point, these are other parts of my life that changed when my outlook did:

- I was hired by The Boston Globe, the largest newspaper of the five I edited (and the one I delivered as a child).

- I finally got a girlfriend (ugh, yes, I was 36!), and later, after 10 years of making up for lost opportunities, I met my special someone and we married.

- The Globe promoted me a couple of times, and I became a section editor for the only time in my career.

- Led by circumstances, Georgina and I chose to adopt.

- On a leap into the unknown, we decided I'd accept a Globe buyout, expecting our adoption to come through within a few months and intending that I'd stay home with the baby for the first three years.

☐ He didn't arrive for almost that long, but when he finally did, I shouldered the greater share of his rearing in conjunction with the most kid-committed full-time-working mother I've ever known.

☐ I completed and published a book, and you're holding my second book.

☐ I'm experiencing the love of child and family that I never anticipated.

Few people would relate any of those results to anything having to do with sustainability, though that's mostly because the vast majority of us have narrowed the concept to the green, or the global. Those two notions definitely fit under the sustainability umbrella, but as a complete definition they're incomplete for this reason:

What's the point of trying to sustain the planet, if we're not trying to sustain ourselves? Clearly, both are needed. If we fail at the former, we'll be homeless. But if we fail at the latter, we soon won't need a home.

The personal sustainability standard is simple: If I were to do [X] every day for the rest of my life, would it enhance or hinder my long-term prospects? Using an example I've already used, it's easy to see that a two-pack-a-day habit is at least doubly unsustainable: Not only does it undermine vitality, who's got $70 a week to spare? But let's consider some others:

- Buying food produced industrially. Factory farming is not a fact of life. It grew and now survives because the vast majority of consumers are willing to purchase its products. If you're one of those consumers, you are quite literally a supporter of this way of doing things, even if you've never once included that in your economic decisions.

  Most people would dispute that they've made that comparison, but that's exactly the point. Our actions have effects, regardless of whether we consider our role in them. Here are some of those effects:

- Inhumane existences for billions of non-humans whose only purpose is to feed us. Obviously there is a food chain, and we see examples throughout nature where one function of those lower on it is to feed those higher on it. But we're the only ones on the chain who have taken away the rest of what a natural existence would mean for all those beings, via gestation crates, vast warehouses that factor out fresh air and sunshine, and excrement-rich feedlots.

▯ Continual degradation of the physical world. Just as we redirect the existences of the animals we eat, we impose our wisdom on other parts of nature, rather than trying to harmonize with it. Healthy soil, for example, is home to myriad organisms that, when allowed, contribute mightily to our well-being. But instead of fostering them, industrial agriculture sees them as threats to be contained. It seeks to accomplish this by using pesticides whose antecedents were chemical weapons, or by modifying organisms so that only they will survive broad and intense applications of a pesticide.

Another example of this degradation includes the aquatic dead zone in the Gulf of Mexico that results from fertilizer running off farms and down the Mississippi River. This dead zone has been measured to be the size of Massachusetts. Yet another example is the vast lagoons of toxic waste that necessarily result from CAFOs — concentrated animal feeding operations. They emit noxious and greenhouse-effect-hastening gases, pollute groundwater, and are often dispersed by being sprayed over nearby neighborhoods.

▯ Yet another feature of industrialized agriculture is the widespread imposition of monoculture, whether among animal breeding stocks (such as turkeys that have been bred for breast meat, to the point of deformity) or among plants bred for easy harvest, or ability to survive long transport. Among the pitfalls of this manipulation of nature is that if the right (or, actually, "wrong") pest develops or is accidentally loosed into a population, it will destroy at will because we have limited the diversity that nature created. Notice that among all these manipulations, nutrition and taste are cast in minor roles, if at all.

You may think these are all necessary and justified for the goals they accomplish. If you have weighed and consciously bought into these manipulations, then quite obviously, we disagree. But my contention is that a) the vast majority of us have not considered the full impact of our actions, and b) if everyone did, the commercial landscape would look far different.

☐ Basing investment only on return. Only a fool invests in losing propositions. But it's also foolish not to consider a company's policies — whom they hire, what they pay, their pollution standards, etc.

As before, many investors would scoff, saying they're not running a social-service agency, but are trying to provide for their families. Fair enough, but this choice isn't one or the other.

And besides, owners are accountable for how their companies run, even if they claim ignorance of their methods.

☐ Engaging in exercise. There are plenty of reasons not to: not enough time, not fun, too tired, other priorities, it's boring, it can be expensive. But no credible set of recommendations addressing vitality, quality of life, or longevity advise against exercise. Whether one wants to exercise is a fact about her or him, but that fact does not change the fact that exercise is an important contributor to good health and quality of life.

There are many more effects, of course; there would have to be in this world of vast, complex interconnection that I'm describing. I speculate that a reason I'm so passionate about this concept is that my introduction to it is one of its most profound examples. Overconsumption is a signature sign of an unsustainable paradigm, and obesity is a signature expression of overconsumption.

The simplest window to see this is the "extra" resources — water, pesticides, artificial fertilizers, petroleum products, and other commodities — needed to produce all that food. But also, do you know many people who eat mostly whole foods who are overweight? It happens, but most obesity results from consuming processed foods, and processed foods are a prime product of industrial agriculture. Deciding to eat more healthfully contributes both to my personal health and to the well-being of the planet.

I find this alignment not only to be divine, but completely, practicably useful. When it presents itself, I can be reliably sure I'm acting in my best self-interest. When it doesn't, I know what to look for.

Discussion/Action Points

Identify a challenge in your life you'd really like to meet but haven't, because you've tried and failed or even been unwilling to try because you're certain you'll fail. It could be improving a skill useful at work, or perhaps cultivating a new approach to a boss or troublesome colleague. How is this lack affecting your physical or mental health and wellbeing? (Choose something changeable according to natural laws; wanting to be 4 inches taller, or faster than a cheetah, doesn't apply.)

How might your outlook or approach to change be keeping you back? Explore whether you want to change, or whether you merely want the unpleasant outcomes of your actions to disappear. Take a good look at your priorities in the matter; are you putting other considerations, perhaps so embedded in habit that you don't notice, ahead of what change would require? (It may be that after examining these questions, you'll conclude that you prefer the status quo, and the benefit you've derived is that you no longer consider it to need alteration.)

Consider additional factors that might be hindering your progress. If the issue is lack of fulfillment at work, for example, one could easily point to factors outside of oneself being to blame. But what internal factors are there, and how can you address them? Consider how you would benefit from changing, apart from pay raises or promotions that might also result.

How does your issue look through the prism of personal sustainability? Do the choices you're making today — regardless of how you explain them — foster your long-term growth? Answer broadly.

If you made the change you desire, how would it affect your own physical health or well-being? How would your aspirations at work be the same or different? In what small or big ways would your change impact your work life, your personal life, your community?

CONCEPT 2

Beyond Just One Thing

An ilk of auto ads goes like this: "The XQ7 has more leg room than a Mercedes, accelerates faster than the Land Rover, and has better gas mileage than a Cadillac." All true statements, but cherry-picked to obscure the basic truth that the XQ7 is a piece of crap that no one would ever think is better than a Mercedes, a Land Rover, or a Cadillac.

Saying something good about something isn't the same as saying something is good.

Food marketers do this, too. Sugary cereals are "high in fiber." Ice creams have "no added sugar." And juice-like kids' beverages are "high in Vitamin C." Even when true, these claims are meant to allow something nice to be said while distracting from the fact that they're promoting sugary cereals, saturated-fat-laced ice creams, and sugar-laden kids' beverages.

But it's never just one thing — saying something good about something isn't the same as saying something is good. Remember, sawdust is very high in fiber.

Start Small

T. Colin Campbell coined this practice as nutritional reductionism in his book Whole: Rethinking the Science of Nutrition. Either as an espouser of green living or as the guy who lost a lot of weight, I encounter the reductionist outlook often. People ask, "What's the one thing I have to do? Whole foods? High fiber? No GMOs? Low fat? No sugar? No flour? No incandescents? No gas guzzlers? Low carb or low fat? Reuse or recycle? Please, what's the one thing?"

The right first step is any first step.

Like those folks, I, too, have wanted the perfect answer, the magic potion, the inside track. But what I stumbled into learning is that (usually) the right first step is any first step.

When I was at one with my couch, I thought about acting differently far more than I actually acted differently. One thing I know now is that change is itself a force of transformation, easing the way for other changes just by its existence.

For example, at a time when I lacked the willingness to work out, a friend suggested I put my workout clothes in the car, without any plan beyond that. And I found myself in the gym soon afterward. The simple act of packing a bag had lowered the hurdle enough.

Journalist Becomes Journaler

When I was in rehab in 1991, I was instructed to keep a journal, for the stated reason that it would allow my primary counselor to sharpen her understanding of my issues and keep tabs on my progress as a patient. Because I'd thought a written record would help me write professionally about my experience later, I'd mused about journaling in the run-up to rehab. But the fact is that I'd considered journal writing for years and never done it, and I question whether I would have acted without the requirement.

During my nine weeks, the journal functioned as designed, but I took the habit with me when I departed. I remained a faithful self-scribe for more than a decade, filling two dozen notebooks before life changes starting crowding the habit out. But just as journaling fulfilled its primary purpose of informing my counselor, it also performed the secondary function of helping me write clearly about the experience, when finally, around 2006, I began writing what developed into my first book, Fat Boy Thin Man.

We frequently take on initiatives that don't do what we want them too, so I feel fortunate that in this case, I gained two results that were designed. But plenty more has flowed from all that ink, none of which I could have foreseen.

　　◻ Most obviously, I became a substantially better writer. I'd become aware early on both that writing came more easily to me than others, and often came out better than most. I wrote my first story for pay while still in high school, and never wanted to study anything but journalism in college. I came to consider that I wrote understandably, which is not nothing, but I never thought I'd move anyone with words or write anything remarkable, either.

　　In retrospect, perhaps I could have seen that consistently working on a craft for more than 10 years would have had to improve my skills.

But not only did I not know it would develop into a daily practice, developing a voice and improving my technique was nowhere on my screen until well after I noticed it had happened.

☐ It rekindled my desire to create. I abandoned the role of writer for editor perhaps a year into my career, because it afforded more regular hours and, I thought, it would not only get me out from under an editor's thumb, it would let me be the thumb. In the decade or so between then and when I entered rehab, I estimate I wrote no more than 10 stories for publication. In the 10 years after, I wrote more than a hundred feature stories; travel articles from Mexico, Cuba, and Kenya; and reviews of magazines, books, and music, both recorded and live. A quirky highlight is that once, on vacation in California, I spent 20 minutes alone in a hotel room with Salma Hayek, while she was promoting her film "Frida."

The epicenter of my creative eruption was a two-page color graphic history of the United Nations that I conceived, wrote, and helped design, pegged to the institution's 50th anniversary in 1995. The project was born of inspiration, a certain lack of good sense, and many long hours shared with my partner on the project, Richard Sanchez.

Partly by luck of timing, it was the first piece ever picked up by the New York Times Syndicate from outside the Times, and it sold to newspapers on three continents, including the Times itself and the hometown Globe.

It clinched the best job I ever had. Perhaps eight years later, well after I'd moved from editing national and foreign news to the feature sections, the Globe devised a series of jobs, one in each department, designed to bridge the gap between the verbal and visual spheres. I grabbed my framed UN history off the wall of my study and brandished it during my interview, and I started two weeks later.

Freed from the routine of copy editing and page layout, I sat in on daily and weekly section conferences covering films, food, life at home, books, television, music, and more, offering ideas on how to add pieces to stories already planned. By design, they were usually small complements, such as the "personal file" interviews that I've continued to do as meatier "10 Words or Less" video interviews on my blog.

But occasionally they were more grand, such as a contest we ran to coincide with a story about Doppler radar coming to the Boston market. I enlisted all the local TV forecasters and pitted them in a weather-prediction competition against one another and a fifth-grade class studying weather, a farmer, and the semi-retired dean of New England forecasting.

Another example was the year we expanded a mail-in contest to see who could outguess our movie critic on predicting the Oscars. Among others we recruited was an anteater that was brought to the Globe photo studio to make his predictions. For each category, we put out a photo representing each contestant dabbed with honey, and wherever the critter licked first constituted the prediction.

As I recall, the farmer, the forecasting legend, and the fifth-graders all avoided finishing last, but the critter didn't.

When an idea was accepted, I then got to carry it through to publication. My contributions got into the paper several times a week, and I left the job only when asked to take over one of the sections I'd been contributing to.

All of that flowered from taking up a pen on direction from my counselor in rehab. Maybe you could have seen that coming; I sure never did.

Beyond One Thing

One last example: When my mother learned that, in my first apartment after college, I was keeping houseplants, she wondered just who this stranger was — the idea that I would be husbanding horticulture was just that foreign to her. Over time, I became a subsistence houseplant farmer, in which it was the plants, not the farmer, that barely got by.

But even with that experience, I had no interest in taking my habit outdoors. Years later, when I took the turn toward sustainability, I still saw no connection between a household hobby and a larger commitment. But now, as a direct result, I'm embarking on my sixth year in a cooperative community garden, an experience I discuss in greater detail in Concept 5.

I know that staying put will take me nowhere.

I raise the point of a first horticulture step here because it illustrates, again, how making one change can lead to others, often totally unexpected and frequently quite valuable. It used to be I would examine every possible outcome and evaluate whether I thought the effort would justify the payoff. Now, I've had too many experiences where a change led to un-expected outcomes — in addition to the expected — to think that I know what's going to happen. Even more important, I know that staying put will take me nowhere.

Discussion/Action Points

Do you relate to wanting the quick fix or the inside scoop? Have you ever taken the quick fix, only to find it leads to more changes?

When have you fought hard to achieve something? When did you achieve or get something (a promotion, assignment, or something of value) without your needing to exert any effort? Generally, which do you value more: What you've earned, or what was handed to you?

When did you follow guidance — enthusiastically or not — that brought unexpected growth or knowledge (regardless of whether you also received an outcome you expected)? For example, your boss asked you to make a presentation to her peers on a project you were working on. Maybe you remember being assigned to document your summer activities for a fall class, and you found it made you a better writer in addition to having the documented memories.

Whom do you rely upon to guide you toward change in your life: a trusted mentor, boss, or co-worker, counselors, teachers, friends, family, or clergy? When have you been willing to take their suggestions, or did you first insist on knowing the intent of the guide and deciding whether the suggestion would work?

Identify a major change you would like to make. Put aside judgments of what seems easy or doable and sketch out the steps required to achieve the change you want. Be fair and thorough, without regard to what you think you're willing to do.

Commit to doing the first step to achieve your major change. Do this for a fair trial period — perhaps a week or a month — and tell a friend or other trusted figure in your life what your issue is, and what your commitment is. Ask for support, but remember that no approval is necessary from anyone.

Sustainable YOU

46

CONCEPT 3

It Matters

Let's start with the obvious question: "It?"

By "it," I mean "everything." Not in an anal-retentive way, not in a self-involved way, but what I do matters.

I make this point because on a planet of 7 billion — and that's only the humans — it's easy to think that what I do, what any one person does, doesn't matter. But that's a misconception — regarding not only planetary but personal change.

The Whole-World View

Consider the notion broadly first. Nelson Mandela did not end apartheid alone, and was not the only force behind South Africa's coming together after it was abolished. But are not Africa and the world substantially different because of this one man? How about Gandhi, who led a nation of 350 million out of colonialism peacefully, while elsewhere in the world, including America, foreign exploiters have been expelled only through war? Clearly, one person makes a difference.

Oh sure, you might say, these were legendary figures, and I'm just one person. To which I say, "Okay, me too." But I'm not talking about doing grand things; I'm just talking about doing something. Even if it's only a seven-billionth share of human output, it's still meaningful.

Another interpretation of the concept lies in what Gandhi once said: "If we could change ourselves, the tendencies in the world would also change." Is that change likely to be enough, to alter the entire world? Of course not. But every change has to begin somewhere, and if I won't change what I can control, how can I expect change to arise at all?

The Personal-World View

If this were only a planet-level view, I'd consider it a tough sell, even though it's entirely true. But perhaps the most fascinating facet of this set of ideas is that when you bring the principle down from planetary to personal, from 7 billion down to one, the value doesn't change. The mundane actions I take in my own life matter — to me!

That might seem like a statement of the obvious, but for my first 30-plus years, I made choices that I somehow maintained were immaterial to my well-being. My eating behavior is the gold-plated example, but I also smoked cigarettes for a dozen years, and ingested other substances I'm better off without.

I frittered cumulative years away watching re-runs of shows I shouldn't have expended time on once, never mind again. I skipped, skimped, and coasted through college, and left after four years still needing two more course credits because I'd blown off easy work in my last semester.

None of them are choices I would endorse today, and certainly none I'd want a loved one to make. If I'd had the perspective I have now, that what I do matters, I believe I'd have made different choices — better choices — more often.

I say "more often" because even today, I'm not perfect by any definition. I still watch TV, or otherwise check out. But here's a way in which the newer perspective plays out: Sometimes, when I see a piece of trash on a sidewalk, I place it in a bin.

Big deal, right? The wind will probably deposit a new piece by morning. And even if not, who's going to notice one less piece of refuse in the world? More or less, I agree with that.

Every Little Bit

But here's the thing: Consider what would happen if everyone picked up stray pieces of litter? No trash, right? What if one in two did? One in four? One in ten? Each of those eventualities would have an effect, and I suggest that's true right down to one.

Ok, maybe that idea is a little quixotic. But I've been picking up scraps of paper, empty coffee cups, and other rubbish for more than ten years, and I haven't quit the practice yet, despite having few clean streets to show for my efforts. But other benefits have accrued. First, there is less trash on the street, even if it's unnoticeable.

Second, taking the action bolsters my self-esteem, at about the same rate the trash is receding, but still: Take a few actions designed to leave a person, or a place, better than you found it and see if you don't feel good about it too.

Third, change is, itself, a force for change. In the context of having my life transformed, I am physically and mentally healthier than I have ever been; married with a child, published author after being dormant as a writer for 15 years, and so on. So street cleaning ranks low in the range. It wasn't my first step toward change, and it wasn't my last. But being open to possibilities, and looking for small ways to contribute, moves me forward.

That's enough for me, especially since I've found negligible downsides to picking up litter. But when I do it, I also have the chance to influence others toward the change I want to see. The fact is, we are all role models. Who hasn't altered a course or shifted dramatically as the result of what they saw someone else do? It could be someone at work who has demonstrated civic responsibility in a corporate context, something your Mom or Dad did, or it might just be some guy you noticed on the subway committing an act of kindness. It might be possible, or it might be that thing you'd never do.

Since, even as just another schmo, I'm going to be a role model, I'd rather it be for something positive.

Since, even as just another schmo, I'm going to be a role model, I'd rather it be for something positive. I think many of us, were we to give it thought, would say the same, but my special motivation arises from understanding, now, how strongly — and usually negatively — I could affect newsroom colleagues when I was in a snit, which was way too often for an adult.

It would be absurd to contend I was unaware, but the effect of my intense anger and hurt was really brought home to me in rehab when I would model that behavior. Unable or unwilling to accept, or acknowledge, or rise above a perceived slight, I would seethe and brood, radiating my displeasure without speaking.

What I wanted was to be rescued, but instead of signaling "injured person needs help," I was silently shouting "angry bastard, stay away." So I would seethe, and those around me would have an elephant in their room, dragging down the mood, or worse, smothering the spirit of communication.

From other newsroom figures, meanwhile, I saw examples small and large about what one person could do. At the Hartford Courant, I worked temporarily for Metro editor Pam Luecke, and one night expressed doubt that I'd be able to fulfill one of her directions.

"You'll be fine," she said. "I trust you."

"Oh, don't trust me until I actually do it," I said.

"No. I trust you until you don't," Luecke said. I'd never even conceived of that perspective, was touched that she did, and will forever have respect and affection for her because of it.

Earlier at the Courant, I'd seen Mike Waller transform the paper whose tagline, "America's Oldest

Continuously Published Newspaper" had been co-opted by wags to be "America's Oldest Continuously Published Newspaper To Never Win a Pulitzer." Unquestionably, Waller's firm but jocular style changed the Courant's course, and inside five years, the Courant had crashed the Pulitzers party.

At the Globe, Marty Baron's effect was even more swift and reached much further. In the previous five or so years before Baron replaced Matt Storin as editor in July 2001, more than 130 victims of pedophilic former priest John J. Geoghan had come forward, but 10,000 pages of church records regarding its conduct were sealed by court order. Where Storin hadn't, Baron fought the confidentiality fiat and won, uncovering a long record of church cover-ups, not only of Geoghan's misdeeds but of many others. The first in the line of stories that altered the Roman Catholic Church forever appeared just six months later.

It's hard to imagine a better example of how one person's actions can transform not only a workplace, but the world.

Discussion/Action Points

Do you believe your actions, small or big, have an effect on your world? Cite an example. Were you try-ing to effect positive change? Or was it by accident? Was it in line with your beliefs at the time? If not, how did it change them?

Have you acted in ways that had a negative impact on the world? How were your actions contrary to or in synch with your beliefs at the time? How did your beliefs change as a result?

Define your self-interest, and then discuss how well or often you act accordingly. How, if at all, do you relate with the observation that many people are willing to give up what they want in exchange for what they want now. Describe some specific ways in which you would act differently if you defined your self-interest beyond whatever feels good or seems expedient.

Do you agree that everyone has been a role model, even if only in small ways? In what ways are you aware of yourself as a role model? Cite examples of when your actions have been influenced by someone else's, both when they were trying (a parent, perhaps) and when they weren't (the last jerk you encountered in traffic). How does recognizing practically everyone's ability to influence others change how you want to act?

Identify a facet of your life where you could consistently do a little more — mentor a colleague whom
you know needs help, even if no one is paying you to
do it; invest more deeply in the quality of your work,
as a statement of your worth to yourself if for nothing else; keep closer awareness on your finances.
Commit to do that. Remember: perfection is not required, although the sages do say, "If nothing changes, nothing changes."

Note: Your effort counts less if you brag about your initiative to others, because it questions whether you're not just trying to score points.

Sustainable YOU

CONCEPT 4

Working Together Is an Act of Self-Interest

For many people, gardening is a solitary hobby, a way to get some time alone in the fresh air. I like being out in the sun, too, but until six years ago, I considered every other reason to be outside better than gardening.

It wasn't just that I didn't get the hobby; I didn't get why anyone did. But then, for reasons having nothing to do with pastime, I built a raised bed for square-foot gardening in my front yard, and it's been paying off for us ever since. That one 6-square-foot box became three boxes the next year, and two years after that, I ditched the boxes to plant the whole plot.

This year, we finally moved into fruit, installing a couple of strawberry plants in a multi-hole planter that was handed down to us. And we've talked about replacing the azaleas in a different part of our yard with raspberry and blueberry bushes.

For vegetables, we have a dozen tomato plants, a half dozen Asian eggplants, more than a dozen pole-bean vines on a trellis, and a handful of singleton varieties. If this is the year we hit it big with tomatoes, we'll make as much sauce as possible, but I'll have no regrets if we end up sharing with the neighborhood.

We water almost exclusively from a rain barrel, and have two composters fed not only by table scraps but from spent grounds and unread newspapers donated by the local coffee shop. I had little knowledge and no technique before I turned in this direction, but I learn more every year.

I also teach, a little, to a class of one. From the beginning, I've been partly propelled to propagate to show my son, who was expected to arrive during that first summer, that food came from the ground before it came to the store. I don't know how long he'll maintain the interest I'm trying to cultivate, but so far (as I write this, he's 3 months shy of 6 years), he's into it. He knows how to pinch the suckers from the tomato plants, wields a wicked weeder, and unfailingly shows more enthusiasm for vegetables in the garden than he ever does on the plate.

As successful as the home plot has been, I've unearthed even more gold at the cooperative community garden that started up in my neighborhood about the time I planted my first square feet. My root reason for joining was to be less of a hypocrite. I'd been espousing green principles, without taking what I thought were enough green actions.

But I was still the last joiner, reluctant to commit to people and to an endeavor I wasn't sure I'd sustain interest in. I don't know what I expected, but here's what I've gained:

- Expertise. We had about a dozen members the first spring, and I was easily the least-skilled and least-informed of the bunch, a status that remained even if you included the fence posts. Now in our sixth year, I'm still gaining not only information, but new approaches and perspectives.

  For example, when a plant fails to thrive on my home land, I have tended just to pull it and move on. In the shared garden, the practice is to assess — often in advance — what else might go into that space for the remaining season, then plant it. We've also divided the lettuce bed into four rows, using succession planting to ensure that we've got fresh lettuce every week.

☐ Sense of community, times two. First, there's the camaraderie inside the fence. I have relationships with many fairly like-minded neighbors now that I wouldn't have otherwise had. In addition, I feel more a part of my town by having a stake in a growing town enterprise. (Or is that town growing enterprise?) If I'm at the playground with my son and see someone peering over the fence, I can invite them in, because I know the lock's combination. I have a sense of belonging.

☐ Support. I probably should have emphasized by now that our garden is cooperative. It's not an allotment garden, in which gardeners are on their own, even if they're making friends over the fences. We not only garden together, we plan it, we propagate it, we blog about it, we even dine together occasionally. One outcome is that unlike the solo gardener, I am free to vacation in summer without worrying about what will befall my rooting interests. Someone will always be watching.

☐ I get outside myself. Working voluntarily in groups allows me to see where I'm strong, and where I'm not. I can also see how others handle challenges that I fumble.

And, not incidentally, there is the food. It's not free. We each pay $75 a year, some of which goes to the town for the privilege of working public land. We keep two-thirds of the fee for ourselves, to pay for seed, implements, irrigation experiments, and other necessities. But we also share a strong recycling ethos: Our trellises are made from bamboo a neighbor is happy to get rid of, and we scavenged our entry arbor and (formerly snow) fence.

I've found that when I was consistently able to make our twice-weekly harvests, they met our family's vegetable needs for a good four months. Work and family priorities have reduced my availability, but the knowledge and resources I have gained from the group clearly have made the home plot more productive. I remain comfortable with the show-up-to-get-your-share arrangement, and even with a smaller contribution to our pantry, all the other benefits continue to make it a great deal for me and our family.

The common view of engaging in community is that, at best, it's a double-edged activity. Even if there are benefits, you have to give up your free time, your free will, and that's hardly the American Way. My knee jerks that way too, which is why I hesitated to join. Now I'm quite pleased that I gave it a try.

Meanwhile, there's an aphorism that goes: If I encounter one jerk in a day, it's probably him. If I encounter a second jerk that day, it might be just poor luck. But if I encounter a third, the jerk is almost certainly me. Sadly, through way too much of my corporate working life, I was the poster crybaby for that story, overly focused on myself instead of more willing to balance group and individual needs.

I grant that going to work every day under threat of homelessness and poverty is greatly different from choosing to join a garden group. But the co-op has allowed me to see the self-interested benefit I get from including group aims in my personal outlook. I don't see it as being less self-interested; I see it as a more robust understanding of what my self-interest is.

Discussion/Action Points

Describe a time where collaborating with others — on a work project, on a sports team, as a volunteer unit — was rewarding, beyond just the task accomplished.

What was your motive for that collaboration? Did you expect to see benefits? Did you experience benefits from the experience that you didn't expect? If yes, describe one or two of them. If not, why do you think that is?

How did the collaboration make you feel? Was this collaboration outside your comfort zone? Were others around you able to benefit from your help or expertise?

List ways in which you are voluntarily in collaboration with others right now.

What new volunteer or collaborative opportunities could you seek out at work (such as organizing a brown bag lunch talk, book club, or other discussion group, working on a team-building project, or creating a lunchtime exercise group for yoga, walking, or running)? What new volunteer or collaborative opportunities could you seek out in your community? If you don't feel you can commit to an ongoing effort, what one-time openings are there?

Sustainable YOU

72

CONCEPT 5

Working Together
Isn't Enough

I started the transformation I've been describing as a lonely isolator, acting to separate myself from others while wishing I weren't so alone. One way I overcame that self-sabotage — not of my conscious design, I assure you — was to join several support communities.

Relating purposefully with others was much better than the self-isolation that came before. But as the Concept 5 title says, it wasn't enough. Its upside is that even if I was still running my show, or attempting to, at least I had input from others. I could follow others' examples, I could ask for help, and I had others to whom I could offer mine. Collectively, at least, we had experience, perspective, even some wisdom.

Consider Who You're Dealing With

But don't forget how I met these people. We all volunteered for group membership because the pain our deficits brought us daily was great enough to seek relief! But even with the group support, we were certainly all humans, guaranteed to err, to have a bad day, to be subject to all manner of pettiness and selfishness.

If relying solely on myself wasn't safe, and neither was relying on a combination of myself and my peers, who was I gonna call? Though I'd wanted nothing of it for decades, it's what a friend calls his deeper power, also known as a higher power or God. I'm willing to use those names, too, but deeper power not only has less baggage for me, it better describes my experience. I experience this power within me, not as external to me.

A Deeper Power

Right about here, some readers may feel disappointed (or worse), as in, "Bummer, I thought there might be something here for me, but now I see he's just another theist, spouting crap I know not to be true." If that's you, I can only say that for years, I related. So before I get specific about this deeper power, I'm going to be very specific about why it must be in this discussion. If I leave it out, I'm leaving out a big part of how I sustain personal change. For me, it's not ethereal or illusive; it's practical.

I hope it will comfort skeptics, nonbelievers, and disbelievers that I have no tie to religion beyond the culture in which I was reared. It's as simple as this:

- When I relied on my own power, I didn't get where I wanted to go.

- When I relied on the strength I found in community, I had more success, but still not enough.

- When I opened, even a crack, to spiritual possibility, I began making progress I hadn't been achieving.

For many years, I had refused even to entertain such a switch because I couldn't bear to be hypocritical — was I just going to flip on one of life's big questions because I saw a selfish angle? Who could respect that? Now I chuckle that in my calculations, the risk of hypocrisy outweighed a chance to be happier and healthier — a chance that has fruited more lushly than I ever conceived.

I was born into a religious tradition my parents firmly believed in. I attended years of religious instruction and worship services. But I left my parents' home militantly and arrogantly opposed to God, convinced both that God was a jerk and didn't even exist. If you think about it, it would require a God-like figure to pull that off: You can't be anything if you don't exist.

My fallacy was exposed in rehab. Afterward, when I kept encountering people who said they were benefiting from seeking spiritual guidance, I eventually had to concede that even if I knew the existence of God was a lie, the seeking of God's will was helpful to many.

When I eventually became willing to do the same, I literally felt constrained by the figurative lack of a burning bush. A friend who'd come from a similar place said he'd finally just made up his own version of God to see if that would help, and he suggested I do the same.

What I came up with was an amalgam of two great-uncles, Joe and Albert. Joe was the brother of my mother's dad, who worked at a low level in a family business. Albert was the brother of my dad's dad, who in small ways filled the void of his brother's death when I was 6. Both had been loving and generous, not only to me, but my siblings as well. They'd sometimes slip me a half dollar or so, but they'd more often just spend time with us. Uncle Joe would take me with him on jobs, to fix a broken window or install a shower stall. He was present the day I learned to ride a bicycle, too.

Neither man had married, which I was sure would be my path. They'd always wanted the best for me, and if I fell short they might be disappointed for me, but I don't recall either even being cross with me. God should be so good, right?

Counter to my hypocritical oath, I quickly came to feel their love as headlights illuminating the best direction for me. I knew it was fake, and yet I felt it was real, as though Albert was on one shoulder and Joe was on the other. I felt more comforted, less alone. That was nice, but I recall when my construct carried into the realm of the concrete.

A number of times after I committed to a clear food plan that included surrendering most processed foods, the gremlins within me that still wanted their bread and circus broke out in other ways. One of the most severe was with sugarless gum, which I equate with strip clubs; both raise hopes they can't consummate. I quickly went from mixing and matching in the checkout aisle to buying several eight-packs a week.

Even worse and somewhat concurrently, I followed my addictive tendency down tobacco road. From ages 14 to 26, I smoked cigarettes up to two-and-a-half packs a day before quitting when Ronald

Reagan doubled the tax from 8 to 16 cents a pack, swearing I would no longer be Uncle Sam's monkey.

But I still allowed the occasional cigar. I'd buy a five-pack for, say, a poker game, and discover three stale stogies in my glove box a month later. I don't recall when that guy morphed into the one buying a box of 50 each week, but that's what I became.

Do the math: That's seven a day! I was letting one extinguish itself on my nightstand at night, and relighting it in the morning. I was arranging my work day to group the tasks I could do away from a computer, so I could sit on the third-floor patio for a smoke break a couple of times a day. I knew none of it was good, or healthy, but I wasn't ready to stop.

One day, I pulled into the tiny lot of my aptly labeled "drug" store, laid No. 50, still burning, in the ashtray, and went in to replenish. I grabbed the Garcia y Vegas and headed for the register, only to find a line I felt too impatient to stand in.

As I cruised the aisles, clutching my score and killing time, I had the thought that Uncle Joe wouldn't want this for me. And just like that, I put the box back in the rack and walked out. By rights, I figured I was entitled to finish the one smoldering in the tray, but I let it go, and I've been free of them, happily, ever since. The funny part of the story is that Uncle Joe smoked cigars every day that I knew him.

I don't know when I stopped traveling with my uncles, but hardly ever do I think of them as active in my life as I used to. Today, I have a spirituality that I not only believe in but can explain — which helps for someone who was so stuck on logic. It begins with realizing that I'm not in charge of the world. Anyone want to argue that?

Then if I'm not in charge, what is? Or, is anything? To me, there's too much evidence of order for the universe to be random, and if there's a design, there's a designer. I think this designer has complete control over its creation, but I differ from many believers on how much control it chooses to exert. Or, perhaps, how it chooses to exert this control.

I used to think that if a supreme being could make everything perfect, but refused to, it was evidence of divine capriciousness.

I used to think that if a supreme being could make everything perfect, but refused to, it was evidence of divine capriciousness. I just couldn't back someone like that. Like so many before me, my flaw was in thinking that I could evaluate the whole, based on seeing only parts of the whole.

Having had much more time to consider, I now see that if everything were perfect, then nothing would be perfect; how does one know good without knowing bad? Also, where's the challenge of living when nothing can go wrong? How does one grow if there's nowhere to grow into? Is not growth one of the recurring principles of the physical world, from youth to old age, from finite to infinite universe?

I think our task in each plane of existence is also to grow. We're in this enormously complicated system in which uncountable outcomes are possible, and our task is to deal with whatever happens. I believe there are immutable principles (be loving, help others, be honest, and so on) and our job is to learn what they are and to put them into action.

> **We're in this enormously complicated system in which uncountable outcomes are possible, and our task is to deal with whatever happens.**

So how does all this speculation constitute a practical argument for relying on my deeper power? At its root, I'm sharing what worked, and that is the essence of practicality. When I was guided by my own lights, I felt utterly lost. When I relied on the lights of others, I fared better but I still encountered situations in which I felt let down by them.

I have removed the habit and training of relying on what appeared, to me, to be a capricious, vengeful God, and replaced it with the belief that I'm on the same footing as everyone else, regardless of birth circumstances. All stations carry challenges. Any circumstance can be improved, or worsened. God isn't out to get anyone or favor anyone. Everyone has something to be learned. And so I can look into each event and try to find what I need to know, or practice what I think I already know, without having to be afraid.

Discussion/Action Points

Read When Bad Things Happen to Good People, by Harold Kushner. It's not very long. Or, at least find a synopsis of it online. Its perspective changed mine, unquestionably for the better.

Do you have a concept of a deeper power personal to you? Describe it. How did you come to believe in this deeper power? If not, describe what keeps you from a belief such as this.

What prevents you from finding a deeper power? What actions might you take to connect you to a deeper power?

How could this deeper power empower you to move forward with changes you would like to make in yourself described in the questions and actions section of Concept 2: The Individual and the Plant: Beyond Just One Thing?

Have you ever known someone from work or your personal life who always wanted the best for you, even if this person fell short sometimes? Give an example.

If you can't think of one, make one up, perhaps mod-
eled on someone who came close. What attributes
does this person have?

How close do you come to being like this, toward yourself? Do you treat yourself as you would treat a loved one?

Commit to sitting quietly for five minutes a day, imagining yourself in the presence of this person of good will. After each session, write a sentence or two about something that arose — an emotion, an inspiration, an intention. Commit to this practice for a defined period, at least a week, preferably a month. After your defined period, describe what, if anything, resulted from your practice. How was it valuable?

CONCEPT 6

Not Everything Has to Make Sense

Which seems more damning: too stupid or too smart? From experience, I'd have to say it's the latter.

My foremost example is my path to spirituality, which I raised in the previous concept, "Working Together Isn't Enough." As I explained, my parents included thorough religious exposure in my upbringing. But at 18 years old, I left their house with no discernible spiritual connection.

This is not to say I didn't have faith. I believed in plenty of things, foremost among them, my ability to analyze, evaluate, and affect. I didn't need no stinkin' white beard in the heavens to tell me what to do; I had it covered.

Root and branch, I was wrong. So it's hard to decide where to begin. But I'll start with this: No fair evaluation of the evidence could have concluded that I had anything covered — except, perhaps, my grimy, thread-worn, misshapen spot on the couch.

Entering my 30s, I had attained a fairly high post at the newspaper where I worked, but soon was busted back in rank because I was unable to work with others. I had yet to connect with even one girlfriend, although I had succeeded in alienating dozens of women while trying. My clothes were worn, ill-fitting rags whose only virtue was shrouding the girth beneath. I had few friends and no intimates, including myself: When asked what I felt, I would tell you what I thought.

How's that for an obvious flaw? I relied on evaluation, and my self-evaluation was horribly lacking.

But there was another flaw as well. On the divide between intellect and spirit — if such a divide exists — I had thrown down on the wrong side. I had evaluated the logic supporting a spiritual life, decided it was unsupportable, and never looked back. Believing in some all-powerful being to explain everything around me was absurd. I had no problem believing not just in the power of logic, but in my ability to apply it flawlessly. Not good.

I had equated spirituality with religion. At best, they overlap; spirituality can exist without religion, and religion without spirituality. Also, I had failed to credit that millions of people had been praying for thousands of years. I saw it, but had explained that obvious fact away instead of seeing if it would work for me.

Perhaps most significantly, I ignored the implications of paradox, which allows that seemingly contradictory conditions can both be true. For me, it is paradoxical that prayer could be illogical and also effective. I looked at Wikipedia's paradox page recently and it lists hundreds of similar impossibilities. Where I once perceived illogic and barred the door, I now see that illogic is not, by itself, reason to reject any idea.

I now see that illogic is not, by itself, reason to reject any idea.

In addition to that, what's a more persuasive proof: that prayer shouldn't work, or that millions of people say it works for them?

My willingness to open myself to the idea of a deeper power was glacially slow to develop, but the pace quickened when I entered eating-disorder rehab in 1991. As I mentioned before, one of the perspectives that jelled during that time was embodied by the question, "If I'm so smart, how did I end up in rehab?" There's something about being institutional-ized that encourages new approaches.

I no longer regard prayer, or other facets of a spiritual life, as political or moral issues. I'm just be-ing practical. My experience is that I am better off when I do it: happier, more willing to change, more loving and supportive — not only to others but to myself.

Is it self-hypnosis? Self-delusion? Outright quackery? Call it whatever you want; I don't care. I did that; now I do this. This is better.

Discussion/Action Points

Can you identify the logical explanation for everything you know or believe? How does this fit in with how you were raised?

Have you ever been convinced you understood a circumstance or condition, only to learn later that you didn't understand it nearly as well as you thought you did? What caused you to change your mind?

Describe a time when you have declined to follow a practice that appeared to work for others, because it makes no sense to you. Did you change your mind? What alternative practice did you find that worked better for you?

Sustainable YOU

CONCEPT 7

If You've Had Enough, Have You Done Enough?

Two of the reactions I get when I enumerate the changes that I've adopted over the years are: "I could never do that" and "Wow, that's a lot." Had the full packet been set before me before I embarked, I would have said the same thing — and I well might have said "forget it!" But looking in the rear-view mirror, I know now that both reactions would have been amiss.

"I Could Never Do That"

The next time you think "I could never do that," about anything, consider the story of Aron Ralston, whose story is told in the movie "127 Hours." After becoming wedged while on a rock-climbing trip in Blue John Canyon, Utah, and realizing he might die, he twisted his arm harshly enough to break his radius and ulna bones, then severed his arm with a dull, 2-inch blade in a process that took more than an hour.

Until the day before he did it, he almost certainly would have said, "I could never do that." But in probably the most extreme illustration of the principle, he forever proved that what qualifies as possible changes according to conditions.

My lesson of this came from changing how I eat, including that I've been chosen not to ingest refined sugar and refined grain for well more than a decade. My opinion is that most people who were ordered to go without one or the other would ditch the grain. But I dropped the sugar without a fight. I fumed and balked about letting go of flour, declaring that it was not a problem for me. In my case, "I could never do that" came out as, "You can't make me do that!"

An independent observer would have seen immediately that I had an unhealthy attachment to flour products, because if the suggestion had been to give up, say, capers, or artichokes, almost certainly I would have gone along — and considered myself lucky at escaping so lightly.

I took another seven or eight years before dropping flour, and then, only when mired in a particularly vicious round of bingeing. I was going through loaves of bread and boxes of pasta, knowing I was in trouble but still proud that even during these times, I didn't go back to the sugar.

My reasons were "complicated" (which is to avoid saying "faulty").

A friend asked if it was possible that gorging on flour products, among other binge foods, was making the overall binges more intense or last longer, and I had to concede, at least, that it was possible. I let myself be led to surrendering flour products as a trial, and I haven't returned to them since. Nor have I returned to bingeing.

This example, and others like it, underpins this concept of "If you've had enough, have you done enough?" When given the suggestion to give up both refined food products, I deigned to do one of them.

My reasons were "complicated" (or more accurately, "faulty"). One, I had awareness that refined sugar was probably not healthy; it is so ephemeral to nutrition that there is no recommended daily allowance for it. RDAs are established for vitamins, minerals, and other nutrients, and refined sugar is none of those. But flour is a staple of bread, the so-called staff of life! Pasta, unless overly tarted up, is a simple repast. How could anyone expect to live in the world without the convenience of sandwiches?

And two, I cared far more about volume than I did about any one substance. If I couldn't get a dozen doughnuts at the only shop that's open late at night, I could still get a dozen bagels.

Now I see that grouping refined sugar and refined grain under the same umbrella makes sense. Both start as natural products of the earth — cane/beets/fruit juice and wheat/rye/corn — which are then mechanically and/or chemically broken into constituent parts. Some portions, including the fiber, are removed, thereby intensifying what's left into a whitish powder.

You may have already noted that the same process, applied to the poppy and coca plants, produces heroin and cocaine. My intention isn't to equate the intensity of sugar and flour with the intensity of heroin and cocaine. But they fit legitimately on a continuum of how processing transforms the effects of simple, natural substances.

"That's a Lot!"

Before I shifted my advocacy outreach from food addiction to sustainable personal change, I found myself a little reluctant to share all the changes I had made for fear I would chase away those who might benefit from my experience. As I conceded at the start of discussing this concept, it's possible that I would have been chased away had someone done that for me.

But with provisos, I see profit in doing just that now. Remembering that I came to these changes grudgingly, fitfully, and often without grace, here are some of the actions I undertook:

- I began therapy — three times, until I hit on a counselor who I'd listen to. (I always give his name, to thank and recognize him: Dr. Robert Deutsch of West Hartford, Connecticut.)

- Under his guidance and other influences, I began considering not only that food addiction was real, but that I might have it.

- I began attending support groups, and later, group therapy.

- I did a bunch of reading as suggested by others who understood what I was trying to achieve. When Bad Things Happen to Good People, by Harold Kushner, was particularly helpful.

- In addition to sugar and flour, I have given up a number of foods that, for my constitution, share the attribute of "never enough." Once I started eating them, I had a hard time stopping. These include popcorn, peanuts, dried fruit, and sugarless candy.

☐ I spent nine weeks in rehab.

☐ I left there with a food plan that included weighing and measuring portions, intent on using those tools only until my ability to estimate healthy portions established itself. (Note: I'm still waiting, all but convinced that that ability is not coming back and wondering if I ever had it.)

Is it a lot? OK, sure, and it's only the beginning of my list, which I provide only to illustrate its extent. No one's list would be the same; for many, it would be very different.

But so what? If you've walked, say, 17 miles after your car breaks down in the boonies, what's more significant, that you've walked "a lot" or that you haven't reached help yet?

I would have been happy if I could have reached my normal-sized body — and the formidable other gains that also materialized — while making less significant changes. Meanwhile, I can fairly say that I did the minimum for my situation: I started with one action, and gradually kept adding until I was getting the results I wanted. I added other actions in the years after, only when I encountered a new hurdle.

More often, I removed actions I'd adopted, when they no longer seemed necessary. When I left rehab, for example, I adopted a kit of disciplines in the service of mindfulness, including not eating while standing up, nor while driving, nor in front of a screen. Though I think those are all good ideas, all those disciplines have fallen away.

For me, and I suspect for most people, the concept of "doing enough" is a moving target.

For me, and I suspect for most people, the concept of "doing enough" is a moving target. What I needed to do at the beginning, what I've needed to do at times since, and what I need to do now are different.

How do I know what I need? By my results. If I'm getting the results I want, then the actions I'm taking are enough. If I'm not, then I need to do at least one more thing, which I can usually identify by a combination of self-reflection and consultation with trusted others.

I can safely give away a practice I think I no longer need, as long as I remain willing to return to it if the evidence suggests I was wrong. I really like what my friend Phil Werdell says: "By remaining willing to do [or redo] anything, I hope I won't have to everything." Me too.

The "Why Should I?" Hurdle

Say someone has a cough, so she takes a lozenge, or some syrup. But it persists, so she goes to her doctor, who tells her she has lung cancer. Now the same person is willing to sit for bombardments of radiation and injections of noxious chemicals. If she's like most people, she'll reorder daily life to meet the threat, and stick with whatever is needed until the crisis passes.

What changed was not her situation, but her understanding of the situation.

That's essentially what happened for me. Intermittently, for years, I thought the problem was my being overweight, and a diet was the solution. I'd tell myself I just had to psych myself up to do it, yet again.

As long as I thought that, why would I try anything else? Each time, when the impetus finally dissipated, I took it as proof of my weakness without ever considering that the method, or even my vision of the problem, was flawed.

In the cancer illustration, the patient needed better-informed judgment from outside herself in order to recognize the nature of the problem, and then to tackle it with appropriate remedies.

I acknowledge the insensitivity of this, even as a metaphor, but a cancer diagnosis does have the "advantage" of being clearly perilous. Even though obesity will also degrade quality of life on the way to shortening it, it rarely rises to the same threat level, making its resolution more optional.

The Better the Reason, the Greater the Hope

Part of the reason I so readily accept the food-addiction concept is that when I conceded that I might be a food addict and began opening myself to the practices, treatments, and attitudes that helped other food addicts to recover, I got better.

Not just a little better, or for just a little while. Dramatically, sustainably better.

At one time, I considered my story as part of the proof that food addiction exists. But no longer. Here is what the facts support:

- I was wallowing in a dysfunction made most obvious by my weight.
- I began thinking and acting differently.
- My life began to transform.

That's a story I can tell without even using the term "food addiction," so maybe food addiction had no role in the transformation. Maybe I bought a ca- nard and happened to get lucky!

No, I don't believe that, and an increasing body of research backs that belief. I pose the straw argument to illustrate its fallacy: Without the possibility that I might be an addict, I never would have begun the sort of "thinking and acting differently" that made the difference. After I accepted I might be a food addict, a new range of remedies came into view, including individual and group therapy, inpatient rehab, and joining support groups.

Please be clear about this. I'm not saying that my path is the only way to lose weight; remember, this isn't just about losing weight. I'm saying that until I began believing that I might have to do more than just cut down on desserts or try the Atkins diet again, I found neither the will nor the way to make the changes I'm now delighted to have made.

The Issue Is Change, Not Food Habits

For you, the challenge may have nothing to do with eating. Say you have trouble staying on task at work. In progression, you might:

- Recognize that the problem recurs, and that whatever declarations or actions you've taken haven't resolved the issue.

- Approach someone you trust, either in your company or a friend in the industry, to acknowledge the trouble you're having, and ask for guidance, direct aid, or perspective on what she or he might do in your situation.

☐ Take action based on the conversation. You don't have to do everything you hear, but if you do nothing, you chose the wrong adviser — or were the wrong advisee.

☐ Inquire with your company's employee assistance program, if there is one, about aid for those with a similar problem.

☐ Pursue whatever remedies you choose in concert with someone else in a similar situation. Alternatively, it could be someone who understands — and takes seriously — the gravity you assign to the problem. In either case, this person is neither above nor below you in the task; she or he is walking beside you.

Just fill in the blanks of what you could do for whatever challenge you have. The point is to take your challenges seriously, overtly commit to change, and seek out support.

In my case, I knew relatively little of what I'd eventually try, and how much of it I would incorporate. But just as surely as there is no one "perfect diet" that's going to please and fix everyone who needs help, the details of change are less important than your motivation.

Discussion/Action Points

To address your foremost work challenge, would you rather have a thorough understanding of it, or, a proven strategy for overcoming it? Why?

When receiving negative feedback, are you more likely to ignore or explain it away, or take steps to address your behavior in the future? If your first stab at it doesn't bear enough fruit, are you more likely to quit trying remedies? Or do you continue to try tactics until you find the change you're seeking?

To resolve a problem, what lengths would you be willing to go if you knew you wouldn't have to do it forever? How far would you go if it was something you would have to sustain?

For any challenge you're facing, make a column of all the strategies you've used to overcome it, and in a second column, evaluate the value of each strategy. Note whether it helped, or how it might have been more effective. Note where you think the strategy was better than your execution of it was.

Below these, list other strategies you might have tried, and note why you didn't. In these cases, did the strategy seem simply too challenging, even if the end result was desirable?

CONCEPT 8

Change Is a Choice

A few times, a parent of an overweight kid has asked me for advice about how to help the child lose weight. And though I do offer an answer, it's not particularly satisfying. On most days, the most effective action might be nothing.

That's because, child or not, if someone doesn't want to change, it's all but impossible to force it.

Externally Imposed Change

I learned this the way most of us learn — through struggle and failure. I was chubby from the start, prompting my mom to suggest (impose) a diet when I was about 10. It was the Stillman Diet, in which I was to drink eight eight-ounce glasses of water daily. She put eight toothpicks on one side of the sink, and with each tumblerful, I was to move a pick to the other side.

My weight was already intertwined with my self-image by then. I hated the attention it got me and cursed it for the experiences I missed out on. I can't recall one thing that being fat was good for.

And yet, there was never a day that I shifted all the toothpicks, and I doubt I ever moved even four in one day.

Other suggested (imposed) attempts followed, escalating to three summers at fat camp, where each year I lost more weight than the year before — because I'd shown up weighing more than the year before. If you can be bundled off to an environment where all your food is controlled and you are made to be active throughout the day, you will lose weight.

But then the summer ends, the fall TV season begins, and the fridge is only steps away. The forces that led to my being a child large enough to need fat camp had not been broached, never mind resolved. Nor had any care program been instituted; confinement was over, and that was supposed to have been enough.

Self-Imposed Change

I don't mean to say that if these elements had been addressed, fat camp would have been a lasting solution for me. Obviously, one can't know such things. What I do know is that despite a couple of 100-pound-plus losses, it wasn't until my 30s that I proved willing to put my desire for change above the conditions required to achieve it. Even then, I was not transformed by a lightning bolt. It was slow, halting change, retarded by the same approaches responsible for where I'd gotten to. I knew better. It was impossible. It was too hard. It wasn't fair.

> **In retrospect, the best I can say is that I had the desire to change before I knew I had it.**

In retrospect, the best I can say is that I had the desire to change before I knew I had it. Why else would I have returned to company's employee assistance program for a third therapist referral when the first two had bombed?

Since then, I've had plenty more opportunities — to take other suggestions, to take new actions based on my own observations, or merely to continue taking the same actions that had been working to that point.

At each juncture, I've had to choose: action or inaction, forward or back. Nothing says that I must do one or the other. Either way, I will experience the outcomes of my actions.

Discussion/Action Points

In your experience, what's the essence of making any change? Identify an instance in which you changed something about yourself. What factors contributed to your success? How difficult was it to make that change? Have you been able to sustain that change?

Have you ever been in the position of not liking a work circumstance, but have clung to it in the face of someone urging you to change it for the better? How has even well-meaning outside influence kept you from making changes that, under other circumstances, you might have attempted? What can that person do to support you in your effort to change?

Have you had the experience of not liking an outcome of your actions, but disliking the apparent solutions even more? Does fear of the unknown under-
cut your willingness not only to attempt the solution,
but to commit to it? What can you do to overcome
those fears?

Identify conditions of your life that you would like to change. (Skip the impossible ones, such as changing your height.) What actions would you need to take to change each condition? What are the advantages and disadvantages to each action?

Would you agree that the most important facet of achieving change is taking action? Not thinking about it, or complaining about it, but acting? If you do agree, how best will you take advantage of this fact?

Afterword

It's my observation that many of us underestimate the value of material change. We see where we are and where we want to go, and base the likelihood of our success on how it seems and feels at the starting point. But upon the first act of change, we are no longer who we were at the start.

It doesn't matter if the change is slight. The erosion was slight at the beginning in Arizona, and now we have the Grand Canyon. No one knew at the beginning what would result, and likewise, neither do we when we make the first change — although I grant that anything measured against the canyon's majesty will seem slight.

My request to you, if you've come this far, is to target a persistent challenge in your life. Devise one change you could make around the challenge and commit to it for 21 consecutive days or more.

Get support for your initiative by asking someone to do it with you, or disclose your commitment to someone and ask if you can check in daily to confirm that you followed through.

Important: Do not regard your action as anything more than it is: one change for a limited period. But also, do not regard it as anything less than it is: a commitment toward sustaining yourself.

Once change begins, you don't know where it will take you. But if you don't change, you know you're not going anywhere.

About the Author

My passion is helping people get well by refocusing on where their own self-interests lie so they can have more power and influence, not only in their intimate world but in the world at large.

My journey to becoming a professional speaker is rooted in a belief in the power to change, born not of faith but experience. I was a fat kid who became an obese adolescent, surpassing 300 pounds for the first time at age 15 and twice more until topping out at 365 pounds at age 33. During that time, I lost more than 130 pounds twice but couldn't keep it off, all the while certain that I knew all I needed to live happily and productively. So why change?

Today, I'm maintaining a 155-pound loss for almost a quarter-century — and consider the second number far more significant than the first. My first book, *Fat Boy Thin Man*, uses memoir techniques to make the case for food addiction as a powerful influence on many lives and on all of society. But I say nothing about dieting and little about food, because I eventually came to understand that weight was "a" problem, but by no means "the" problem.

Professionally, I was a daily newspaper journalist for 30 years, most recently editing for 14 years at the Boston Globe. Additionally, my writing on a range of topics and in the forms of news and feature stories, reviews, and op-eds has appeared in dozens of newspapers and a number of magazines.

My combination of decades of storytelling practice and decades' worth of a unique, personal, and inspirational tale to tell situates me to share my journey's implications with all who want to achieve and maintain healthy, personal change of their own.

I am blessed with a wife, Georgina, who believes both in me and my mission to communicate this message, and a son, Joseph, who is nothing less than a gift of fate. We live together in Arlington, Massachusetts.

Collaborate with Michael

Sustainable You: Align what you do with what you really want

Michael's primary mission is to present ideas, inspiration, and practical help on a question vital to all: How can we best sustain ourselves to find and enjoy the present and future we want for ourselves, our families, our enterprises?

Although the mission is focused, he shares them in a multitude of ways ranging from groups of any size to one-on-one sessions. Each offering is complete as a sole endeavor, but as client needs warrant, combinations of these offerings can work to effect and sustain long-term change.

Keynote

An interactive presentation with opportunities for customization to client needs, ranging from 30-75 minutes.

Seminar/webinar

Half-day events use the Sustainable You workbook to explore Michael's 8 "Concepts of Personal Sustainability." They are a mixture of presentation, individual reflection, group exercises and group sharing.

Group coaching

One of Michael's tenets is the importance to self of engaging in community, and one way to experience its benefits is to pursue coaching within a group. Support comes from each other, and many of the best lessons come from peer experience and observation.

Individual coaching

Michael has completed the Wellcoaches training, in which the client leads the way, setting the vision for change, determining the order of battle, and building upward momentum via achievable first steps.

Fat Boy Thin Man: Get off the yo-yo at the low end and stay there

All of Michael's professional outreach arises from his decades of obesity and his decades of escape from its worst outcomes. Although he now presents most often on the broader implications of his transformation, a number of clients still ask for help and guidance out of that morass specifically.

Keynote

So much of what we understand or believe regarding our food choices is wrong, both at the individual and system levels. This presentation bares many of these faults, identifies their origins, and helps each listener determine the changes that will be most meaningful for them.

Group coaching, individual coaching

As a follow-up to the keynote, or as discrete offerings, both forms of coaching program help to achieve, and more importantly, to sustain healthful lifestyle changes.

Other services

Before Michael published his first book, he worked for 30 years in daily newspaper journalism. Since then, he has helped found and has worked with several food-addiction advocacy groups.

- **Event host**
- **Panel moderator**
- **Interviewer**

See a list of clients, and their reactions to working with Michael, at MichaelPrager.com. To inquire about an event for your group, or about coaching programs, call or send email:

- 781-951-2411
- office@michaelprager.com.